02

Preface

By me..., Rob

Hi, so I am a digital media technical tutor at the University for
the Creative Arts, a mixed media designer and maker, and who
has been diagnosed with dyslexia. I was tempted then to put
sufferer, but I don't feel that is something I suffer from, yes,
it's a pain in the ass, and yes it takes more time to read some
text. Yet dyslexia gives the advantages of creativity and the
ability to explain things in different and alternative formats.
It has changed my life and the way I overcome problems,
as well as the way I tackle teaching difficult programmes to
students of a range of ages.

My dyslexia is one of the first things I say about myself, when
I start teaching. Yes, I'm bald, gay, gorgeous and a bit
delusional, but I think my dyslexia is the most interesting thing
on the list. Being open gives me more time to learn names
and relaxes my anxieties about writing on the screen/ board
and reading the names of things, mainly fonts. It turns out I
incorrectly named a font in my classes for over a decade, and
no one corrected me. I mean, who is going to recognise the
difference between "Apple Chancery" and Apple Chemistry;

I mean someone might, but not me. Being open about my dyslexia not only gives me a bit of breathing time, it also offers the ability for an open dialogue about dyslexia, reading, writing and accessibility with the intent to foster an accepting community of practice.

The support I received over my time studying my BA, PGCE, HEA and now as I undertake my MA in Visual Communication has been life-changing. Hand on my heart, I can say that if I did not have this support I would not be where I am now.

Now... to this book, it's has come out of research I did for my PGCE and MA, and my goal is to pass on some of the anxiety that comes with dyslexia when asked to read a piece of text, either in your head or out loud. This was an activity I had to do for GCSEs, where we all took turns to read paragraphs of Stone Cold by Robert Swindells, and on my BA when we were asked (forced) to read a section from my dissertation to a group.   This filled me with anxiety and the latter led to me having small panic attacks. Often this task for a student without dyslexia is stressful and even more so for some with dyslexia (nearly said suffers again). The aims of the book and how it is intended to be used and read are explained on the next pages, or it might just be some nice-looking images that aredifficult to read! Either way I hope it gives you the neurodiverse reader some guidance and the neurotypical reader an empathetic perspective.

Contents

08

Introduction

Into

After conducting primary research on how dyslexia and those with reading difficulties affect individuals when reading the written word, this book uses the prologue from Romeo and Juliet for two reasons. One of the reasons is that there is an expectation for English literature students to be 'forced' to read it in classes, usually out loud. This can cause stress and anxiety for people with dyslexia, as someone with dyslexia, I know this feeling all too well. Secondly, the selection was made because the works of Shakespeare are in the public domain and easily accessible.

The goal of this book is to create a sense of stress and anxiety in the reader who does not have dyslexia and to show those with dyslexia that they are not alone in their struggles with text. To add to the stress and anxiety, there is a small test at the end of the book based on the KS4 GCSE revision that students undertake.

10
AR

How AR works within this book

There are Augmented Reality (AR) elements throughout this book,
using Adobe Aero. These elements allow the reader to scan
the QR codes on certain pages, offering an animated visual
response that can be played over the printed page within
the book. This includes moving images with audio examples.

*Avalavle on iPhone and on Android, as the point that this
publicaion was written, it was in beta testing

How to use AR

Scan the QR code on the page

Open Adobe Aero

Once the Aero document has loaded align the trigger on the page to load the content

14
Submissions

How the primary research was undertaken

My primary research took the form of a survey which was shared on Instagram, this was used to collect the written accounts of what written text does to a reader, with reading difficulties. I am going to use both still and moving digital manipulation to mirror the experiences of the dyslexic reader. This will be done by animating, stretching, shadowing, etc. showing the reader's view.

To collect examples of the different styles of dyslexia, reading difficulties and the effects they have on the written word, I conducted an online survey which was shared on Instagram.

I kept the questions simple:

1. Do you find you have issues when reading printed
   or digital text?

2. Do you consider yourself to have dyslexia?

3. Have you ever been diagnosed with dyslexia?

4. In your own words, what does the text do when
   you are reading?

My hope was, to keep the questions simple and give the
participants the ability to explain what the text does to them
when reading. The research does not show all the ways text
can be presented as this is very personal to each individual
and out of the scope of this poster display. Using the answers
from the survey I am creating a range of visual responses
to them to show some of the ways the individual is affected.
With the hope of showing the different ways, text can affect
those who are non-dyslexic from their experience and told to
me in their own words.

18

Example
one

"I often confuse letters when reading, having I J K L B & D all
    swapped around and moving on the page."

"Confusion of letters and movement of words."

"Read letters as flipped or distorted, like I mix up d's and b's and
    p's and Q's words lose their individuality and all look similar."

Working with the Garamond font as a base, I have manipulated
    it by flipping letter forms and swapping similar letter forms
    with each other, creating an almost illegible font. If you know
    the text, you might be able to decode it, but it would take a
    long time and be very difficult.

Two households, doth alike in dignity,
In fair Verona, where we lay our scene,
From ancient grudge break to new mutiny,
Where civil blood makes civil hands unclean.
From forth the fatal loins of these two foes
A pair of star-cross'd lovers take their life;
Whose misadventured piteous overthrows
Do with their death bury their parents' strife.
The fearful passage of their death-mark'd love,
And the continuance of their parents' rage,
Which, but their children's end, nought could remove,
Is now the two hours' traffic of our stage;
The which if you with patient ears attend,
What here shall miss, our toil shall strive to mend.

22

Example
two

"Blocks of text sits on a page, depending on the colour of paper
it changed. Thin fonts are hard to read."

I have manipulated the letter forms from the font Garamond by
making them thinner, along with elements missing from their
form. In the animation, I have incorporated the visual effect of
bleaching on blocks of text and included the decoding of text
on a coloured background.

Two households, both alike in dignity,
In fair Verona, where we lay our scene,
From ancient grudge break to new mutiny,
Where civil blood makes civil hands unclean.
From forth the fatal loins of these two foes
A pair of star-crossed lovers take their life;
Whose misadventured piteous overthrows
Do with their death bury their parents' strife.
The fearful passage of their death-marked love,
And the continuance of their parents' rage,
Which, but their children's end, nought could remove,
Is now the two hours' traffic of our stage;
The which if you with patient ears attend,
What here shall miss, our toil shall strive to mend.

26
Example
three

"When I read to much my eyes kind of dart away from the text
   in reading."

For the eye dart, I have animated the text to dart and drift away,
   leading to a blurred mass.

SCAN ME

Two households, both alike in dignity,
In fair Verona, where we lay our scene,
From ancient grudge break to new mutiny,
Where civil blood makes civil hands unclean.
From forth the fatal loins of these two foes
A pair of star-cross'd lovers take their life;
Whose misadventured piteous overthrows
Do with their death bury their parents' strife.
The fearful passage of their death-mark'd love,
And the continuance of their parents' rage,
Which, but their children's end, nought could remove,
Is now the two hours' traffic of our stage;
The which if you with patient ears attend,
What here shall miss, our toil shall strive to mend.

30

Example
four

"Also I find I have to read things multiple times as the
information completely disappears after I have read it."

To show the need to read things multiple times, I have layered
fragmented pieces with different opacity. As you read through,
the text becomes progressively easier to read.

Two hous   alike in dignity,
In fair Verona, where   e lay our scene,
From ancient   dge break to new mut   y,
Where c il blo   kes civil hands unclean.
From forth th fatal l ns of thes   wo fo
A p   of star-cross'd lovers take the   ife;
   hose   adventured p teo   ov   rows
Do with their death bury thei parents' strife.
Th fear ul pa   ge o th ir death-mark'd love,
And the c ntinuan e of their p   nt   ra e,
Which, but th r children' en   nou t cou d r m e
Is now he two hours traffic of o r stage;
The which if you w h p ient ears at nd,
Wh   here sha l miss, our to l sha striv t m

34
Example
five

"What I think it reads, it does not. Only when I get corrected I
    can see I've read it wrong."

For this, I have rewritten the prologue, attempting to replicate
    the mistakes I usually make when typing or writing a block of
    text, only to have them highlighted in red and shown to me the
    mistakes I had made.

Two households, both alike in digniy,
In dair Veriona, weir we laie out scene,
From acint grude beakes to new muntiny,
When civli blood makes civil hands unclean.
From foth the fatle loins of thse tow foes
A pair of srar-crosd lovers take there life;
Whose misadvanturd pireus overthrows
Do with their death bury there prrients strike.
the ffeaful passage of their dethmaked love,
and the continuacaen of there pariens range,
which but there chidrens end, nought could remvoe,
is now the tow hours trafic of your stage,
The wich if your with parients ears attend,
What here shall miss our toil shall srtive to mend.

38

Example six

"Either they blur together or I confused letters with others or I read it as a completely different word. Another thing is they all band together so I can't see what letters and grouped together and change to make a word."

For this example, I focused on the blurring together of letter forms. Additionally, I have used the flipped font and a stretched letter forms font that I have developed.

Tuo households   both alike jh bjghjty,
Jh fejr Ucrohe, where we ley ovr saehe,
Froh ancient grudge break to heu hvtjhy,
Where civil blood makes   ajujl nehbs vhaleeh.
From forth the fetel lojhs of these two foes
A qejr of ster-aross'b louers teke their life,
Whose misadventured piteous overthrows
Co ujtn tnejr beetn bury tnejr parents' strife.
The feerfvl qessege of tnejr beetn-herk'b. love,
And the continuance of their qerehts' rege,
Which,   dvt tnejr children's end, hovgnt could rehoue,
Is now tne tuo novrs' treffja of ovr stege;
The unjan jf yov with patient ears attend,
Vnet here shall miss,   ovr tojl shall strive to hehb.

42

Example
seven

"The letters jiggle and wiggle if it's black on white.

I have Irlens syndrome too which was discovered during

my dyslexia diagnosis."

"It swirls and swims like a river."

"Moves around and looks like word soup."

For this example, I have selected a range of words from the

prologue and made them move randomly, blurring together.

SCAN ME

Two **households.** both alike in dignity,
In fair Verona, where we lay our scene,
From ancient grudge break to new mutiny,
Where civil blood makes civil hands unclean.
From forth the fatal loins of these two foes
A pair of star-cross'd lovers take their life;
Whose misadventured piteous overthrows
Do with their death bury their parents' strife.
The fearful passage of their death-mark'd love,
And the continuance of their parents' rage,
Which, but their children's end, nought could remove,
Is now the two hours' traffic of our stage;
The which if you with patient ears attend,
What here shall miss, our toil shall strive to mend.

46
Example
eight

"Words combine together, so like a weird hybrid. Another thing
   is the words dance and change order completely. I'll have
   to re-read the same sentence three times to even begin to
   understand it. It has to be spoken as I read it to understand."

Visual interpretation

One of the ways I manipulated the base typeface was to stretch
   out the letterforms and decrease the spacing between letters,
   which joined together to create hybrid words. I have included
   a voiceover from the main text-to-speech software supplied
   by DSA to help decode the prologue.

SCAN ME

Tuo households, dotn alike in dignity,
In fair Verona, uncrc uc lay ovr sachc,
Froh ancient grudge break to new mutiny,
Vncrc civil blood makes civil nehbs vhalceh.
From forth tnc fatal loins of these two foes
A qejr of star-cross'd lovers take their life;
Vnosc misadventured qjtcovs overthrows
Do with their death bury tncjr parents' strjfc.
Tnc fearful passage of tncjr death-mark'd love,
And the continuance of their qerchts' regc,
Vnjan, dvt tncjr children's chb, nought could rchouc,
Is now the two hours' traffic of ovr stegc;
The which if you with patient ears attend,
Vnet here shall miss, our toil snell strive to mend.

50

Example
Nine

"Letters and words move around and some words my brain can't compute and then to even start trying to figure how they are pronounced."

For this example, I have created an animation where the letters swap and move from a readable font to a swapped and flipped typeface I have developed.

SCAN ME

Two households, both alike in dignity,
In fair Verona, where we lay our scene,
From ancient grudge break to new mutiny,
Where civil blood makes civil hands unclean.
From forth the fatal loins of these two foes
A pair of star-cross'd lovers take their life;
Whose misadventured piteous overthrows
Do with their death bury their parents' strife.
The fearful passage of their death-mark'd love,
And the continuance of their parents' rage,
Which, but their children's end, nought could remove,
Is now the two hours' traffic of our stage;
The which if you with patient ears attend,
What here shall miss, our toil shall strive to mend.

54

Example ten

"Block capitals: my brain sees these as an image and I have to really concentrate to read it as words- I need to see the shape difference in the lowercase script to identify words fluently. All text blurs as I am reading."

I manipulated the font in this example so that capital letters that looked similar would be the same. This gradually progressed into the standard font in all caps with tight letter spacing, and eventually evolved into upper and lower case, making it more legible.

SCAN ME

TVQ EQVZEEQJGZ, BQJE AJJKE JM DIGNITY,
JM EAJP VERONA, VEEPE VE JAY QVP ZGEME,
EPQM AMGJEMT GPVGGE BPEAK TQ MEV MVTJMY,
VEEPE GJVJJ BLOOD MAKES CIVIL HANDS VMGJEAM.
EPQM EQPTE TEE EATAJ JQJMZ QE TEEZE TVQ EQEZ
A PAIR QE ZTAP-GPQZZ'G JQVEPZ TAKE TEEJP JJEE;
VEQZE MJZAGVEMTVPEG PITEOUS QVEPTEPQVZ
GQ VJTE THEIR GEATE BVPY TEEJP PAPEMTZ' ZTPJEE.
TEE EEAPEVJ PAZZAGE QE THEIR GEATE-MAPK'G JQVE,
AMG TEE CONTINUANCE QE TEEJP PAPEMTZ' PAGE,
VEJGE, BVT TEEJP GEJGPEM'Z EMG, MQVGET GQVJG REMOVE,
JZ NOW TEE TVQ EQVPZ' TRAFFIC QE QVP ZTAGE;
TEE VEJGE JE YQV VJTE PATJEMT EAPZ ATTEMG,
VEAT HERE ZEAJJ MJZZ, QVP TQJJ ZEAJJ ZTPJVE TQ MEMG.

58

Summary / outro

Outro

I am certain that this publication hasn't shown everything that
text can do, and I never expected it to. However, I hope that
it has demonstrated what text might look like for someone
who has dyslexia.

Soooo... to the test, there is not one, but hopefully, you felt the
added stress while reading this book. However, if you did
want to test your knowledge from what you have read, BBC
Bitesize has a test where you can take a short test used for
KS4 GCSE revision.

As an educator, it is crucial to empathise and put yourself in
your student's shoes to identify any barriers to learning they
may face. Now dyslexia is more recognisable, however, people
often spend time trying to help individuals cope without fully
comprehending its impact. My hope for this publication is to
provide the reader with a better understanding of what your
students may experience when asked to read text (hopefully
not out loud to a class, unless they want to).

60
Suggestions

Suggestions

The ways in which we teach and educate our students are continuously developing as we understand the different ways in which they learn and how we can best support them to reach their full potential. We must continually reflect on how we can minimise barriers to learning. In this session, I have listed some simple good practices for making the written word more accessible.

Difficulty readers might face.

Understanding comprehension and meaning.

Time taken to complete the reading, leading to needing extra time.

Students can find reading frustrating, leading them to lose confidence and self-esteem.

Slow processing of the text.

Phonological difficulty.

Writing

Short, simple, direct sentences.

Clear instructions.

Use active voice.

Avoid double negatives.

Be concise.

64

Fonts.

Veranda or Arial (use these as they are evenly spaced) This publication uses Lexend, which is a free font that is available on Google fonts and is designed to be easy to read.

10-14pt

Dark text on a non-white background (preferably soft pastel)

Do not use primary colours as backgrounds as these colours are difficult for people with colour blindness to read. This is why this publication is offered in a range of pastel colours. One is pastel pink; this is my preferred colour for ease of readability.

Lexend (10 pt, 18 pt line spaceing)

abcdefghijklmnopqrstuvwxyz.

ABCDEFGHIJKLMNOPQRSTUVWXYZ.

1234567890.

The quick brown fox jumps over the lazy dog

66

Lay out.

Justify text left.

Avoid using narrow columns.

Use short lines of text and short sentences.

Lines spacing of '1.5' more grater.

Avoid starting new sentences at the end of a line.

Use bullets and numbers.

Headings.

Avoid underlining and italicising text.

Make text bold instead.

Avoid block capitals.

Make headings larger than the body text.

Separate sections of the text into boxes or borders around them.

68

Use simple charts and graphs to show the information (e.g. flow charts to show procedures).

Use lists (e.g. for instructions, 'Dos and Don'ts').

Keep it simple.

If you are creating long documents use a contents page at the beginning of the document and an index at the back. Making navigation of the document simple.

Giving students a vocabulary list to help with the reading.

Printed in Great Britain
by Amazon

43457431R00040